PUTTING

Anger to Work

FOR YOU!

PUTTING

Anger to Work

FOR YOU!

Ruth Schroeder
Joel Schroeder

SKILLPATH® PUBLICATIONS
MISSION, KANSAS

Editor: Kelly Scanlon

Cover and Book Design: Rod Hankins

Library of Congress Catalog Card Number: 95-69000

ISBN 1-878542-86-9

Printed in the United States of America

Table of Contents

INTRODUCTION

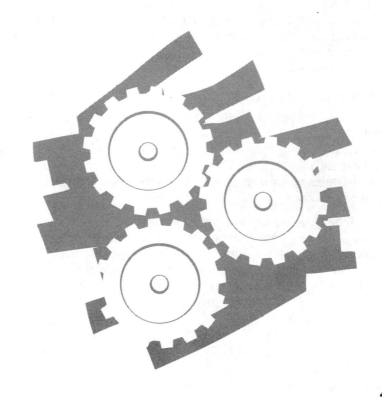

> *Anita saw Fred stalk out of the boss's office, fists clenched,*
> *and disappear into the copy room. As the boss hurried*
> *across the hallway, Jimmy, the office messenger, collided*
> *with him. The boss, red-faced, dressed Jimmy down for*
> *not watching where he was going. Anita gritted her teeth,*
> *feeling her frustration—and anger—rise. She knew*
> *that given the morning's events, there was no way she*
> *could approach the boss for the raise she knew she was*
> *entitled to.*

Anger is everywhere in our world. And it seems to be contagious.

We can take comfort from the fact that basically there are only two kinds of anger: your anger and other people's anger. As you work through this book, you'll first look closely at your anger—what it is, where it comes from, and what you can do to make it work for you. Then you'll learn methods and techniques you can use to deal with others' anger, both at home and at work.

WHAT IS ANGER?

Without some kind of outside indicator, it would be impossible to tell whether you're angry or in love. The physiological condition is the same in both situations—butterflies in the stomach, rapid heartbeat, shallow breathing, and dilated pupils. These physiological changes take place in the initial stages of any strong emotion. Together, these changes are called the stress response.

Research on the stress response has shown that in a perceived emergency, the body's pituitary-adrenocortical system releases the hormones necessary to cope with the threat. The body shunts blood away from the skin and digestive system into the heart, lungs, and skeletal muscles. These physiological changes enable you to run faster, hit harder, endure more pain, and generally do whatever you must do to survive the threatening situation.

But in our modern world, what stimulates the response often is not something that hitting harder, enduring more pain, or running faster will resolve. Biologically, anger prepares you to defend against an assault or threat to your survival. But instead of lions and tigers and bears (oh my!), you face bills and bosses and bureaucracy (oh my!).

Emotions are simply the labels we give to the bodily reactions triggered by the stress response, based on our knowledge of the situation and the circumstances. For example, if you're experiencing a stress reaction and you just got fired, you assume you're angry. You've attached a label, anger, to a certain physiological state, based on your knowledge of the situation. In short, in order for you to be aware of your emotions, you must at some level be aware of your body. The more out of touch you are with your body, the more out of touch you are with your emotions, and vice versa.

In her book, *Emergence, Labeled Autistic*, Temple Grandin explains how she developed an unusual apparatus to calm herself. She noted that cattle became calm when they were held firmly in a chute during physical examinations or when they received shots. Theorizing the same kind of device might benefit people, she designed what she calls a "squeeze machine." When she puts her whole body in the machine and applies firm pressure, she becomes calmer. She's also found that she's able to relate better to people. Being held firmly has allowed her to become more emotionally attached because she is more in touch with her own body.

FEEL YOUR ANGER!

Some people believe that anger is wrong and we shouldn't feel it. Others believe that we should openly express anger in all situations. Neither extreme is correct. Major research on anger has shown that people who are most prone to vent their rages get more angry, not less angry. On the other hand, many maladies have been linked to repressed or suppressed anger. In *The Angry Book*, Theodore Isaac Rubin lists hypertension, heart disease, infections, colitis, and ulcers among the undesirable consequences of repressed anger.

We need a middle ground here. Feelings, in and of themselves, are neither right nor wrong. And we don't always have to act on them. Angry feelings are not angry actions. Anger is not synonymous with hostility or aggression. Rather, hostility and aggression are ways to express anger.

CAN SOMEONE MAKE YOU ANGRY?

The popular saying "No one can make you angry—you make yourself angry" is true and not true. Certainly, we must each take responsibility for our actions. We must be responsible for managing our own anger, but so too must the person delivering the insult, manipulating you, or "attacking" you.

In this book, you'll learn how to use anger to your advantage, to make your stressful situations *better*. Anger is a tool you can use for good. It's not something to repress, deny, or fear. Read on to learn the secrets of putting anger to work.

1

Is Anger *Your Friend or* Your Foe?

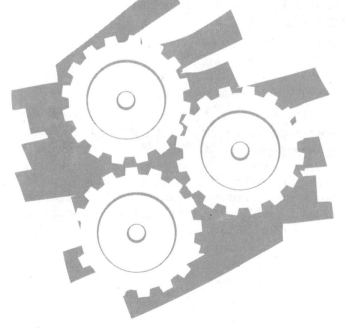

Is anger your friend or your foe? The answer to that question is "both." Anger is a friend, warning you of danger and allowing you to mobilize your strength to combat a threat. But anger is also a foe, destroying your health and relationships. How you handle your anger is something you have learned over many years. Have you learned to use it as your friend, or as your foe?

ANGER, YOUR FRIEND

In practical terms, anger is to your psychological self what pain is to your physical self—a warning that something is wrong and needs attention. Anger is an alarm that tells you when a personal boundary is being violated or threatened. In this way, anger is your friend. There are three major situations in which anger plays a good role:

1. As the protector of your self-worth
2. As the guardian of your convictions
3. As the announcer of your unmet needs

GUARD YOUR SELF-WORTH!

When you are deprived, exploited, manipulated, frustrated, betrayed, or humiliated, your self-worth is threatened. You get angry. Anger alerts you: You are being violated! Anger provides you with energy to act.

Too often society blames the victim. A woman is raped—she shouldn't have been dressed that way, out at that time of night. A person is stabbed during a mugging—he shouldn't have been in that part of town, alone. In those types of blaming situations, it's easy for the victim to know that his or her self-worth is under attack. But attacks on self-worth are often more subtle. Sometimes you may not even realize you are a target, particularly when the attack involves subtle *verbal* aggression. You may even tend to blame yourself in these situations.

You may tell yourself, "I am too sensitive ... too childish." But in fact, you are under the attack of verbal abuse. "Even John understands this point" doesn't sound the alarm bells it should. The underlying premise is "John is very stupid. But even stupid John understands this. You don't because you are more stupid than John."

RIGHTEOUS ANGER

Besides being the protector of your self-worth, anger is the watchdog of your convictions. Here, what many call "righteous" anger comes in— anger against injustice. When you see a child being beaten or a person benefiting from wrongdoing, anger propels you to do something about it. Again, anger provides energy.

ANGER UNDERSCORES UNMET NEEDS

Anger is also your friend when it compels you to do something about your unmet needs. These may be real or perceived needs. For instance, you need food, clothing, and shelter, but if your job does not pay enough to meet those needs, you will be angry. And if you feel trapped in that job, then more than likely you will experience chronic anger.

Often people get angry when they are afraid. Thus the threat of downsizing may bring feelings of fear masked as anger. Fear in the heart jumps from the tongue as anger. When you realize that the source of your anger is fear, and when you deal with the cause of your fear, anger will dissipate.

In all of these situations, anger can be your friend. But you must recognize your anger and use it to motivate you to take constructive steps to change the situation. If you don't, your anger will fester and you will only experience more anger.

The exercise on the next page presents several common scenarios. As you read each one, determine the underlying source of anger. Identifying the source is the first step toward understanding anger and using it for your benefit.

Exercise 1:
WHAT'S THE SOURCE OF YOUR ANGER?

Identify what is happening in the following examples. Is self-worth being threatened? Are convictions being challenged? Are needs not being met? Circle S for self-worth, C for convictions, or N for needs. You may circle more than one letter if you think more than one factor is playing a role in the situation.

S C N   1. Your boss won't listen to your ideas to save money.

S C N   2. Your company publicly claims to listen to customers, but in practice it doesn't.

S C N   3. An employee who reports to you performs only when forced.

S C N   4. Your company compensates workers far below what they need to live.

S C N   5. A double standard exists between salaried and hourly workers in terms of privileges offered. You are an hourly employee.

S C N   6. Other supervisors won't cooperate with you.

S C N   7. Your boss micromanages and won't empower employees.

S C N   8. You have too much work to do for the amount of time you're given to complete it.

S C N   9. You hear rumors that your company is downsizing and you may lose your job.

S C N 10. Your staff complains and resists your management approach.

S C N 11. Employees bring personal problems to work and don't do their jobs well. You end up with more work.

S C N 12. Your boss has a negative attitude.

S C N 13. You've just attended another boring two-hour meeting that leaves you feeling unproductive.

S C N 14. Management often lies about workplace situations.

S C N 15. Your boss, who is a perfectionist, gives you back your report for a third edit.

S C N 16. Another supervisor failed to submit part of your big project. He is procrastinating again.

S C N 17. Your supervisor criticized you severely for last month's performance, even though you put in extra effort.

S C N 18. Your partner is complaining again that you don't do enough around the house.

S C N 19. You work in a family business run by incompetent family members.

S C N 20. You are a union member, and management is playing hardball on contract negotiations.

S C N 21. You have no hope to advance in your company although you are making a great contribution to the company's success.

S C N 22. On the night before her geometry final, your daughter puts off studying and then asks for your help at 10 o'clock.

If you marked more Ss than Cs or Ns, you may be angry because your self-worth is being threatened.

If you marked more Cs, check whether you are angry because your opinions and convictions aren't being heeded, by you or by others.

And if you marked more Ns, ask yourself this question each time you become angry: Is this anger a signal that my needs aren't being met? Then identify what those needs are and begin a plan to meet them!

ANGER, YOUR FOE: THE DOWNSIDE OF MISHANDLED ANGER

Chronic anger can kill. When you allow anger to become a dominant emotion in your life, you slowly destroy yourself—and often those around you. In addition, anger can interfere with your ability to concentrate and to solve problems.

If you anger easily and often, you may have a Type A personality. People with Type A personalities often have stress-related difficulties—ulcers, colitis, high blood pressure, and heart disease. Attempts to put an artificial lid on anger can lead to anxiety, depression, insomnia, psychosomatic illness, alcoholism, frigidity, and impotence.

The interpersonal costs of chronic anger are just as great. Anger leads to isolation, diminished satisfaction with life, and loneliness.

Why?

Because anger feeds on itself. When you act aggressively toward others, they may react aggressively towards you. Left unchecked, these responses can become a vicious cycle.

In fact, Albert Bandura, author of *Aggression: A Social Learning Analysis*, notes that even watching aggression increases hostility and acting out in the person watching. The more you're angry, the more you're angry.

So, when is your anger a friend and when is it a foe? Anger is your friend when you use it to work toward a solution. It is your foe when it tears up you or others. In Exercise 2, you'll get an idea of whether you're allowing anger over life's nuisances to build up inside of you.

Exercise 2:
WHEN DO YOU GET ANGRY?

Place a check mark next to each statement that applies to you.

☐   1. I get angry when traffic jams up and I'm late for work.

☐   2. I get angry when a jerk cuts in front of me on the interstate.

☐   3. I get angry when my partner forgets to turn the lights off and wastes electricity.

☐   4. I get angry when a telephone call from my mother interrupts my favorite television show.

☐   5. I get angry when my three-year-old spills her milk for the second time in a week.

☐   6. I get angry when I try to pay the bills and the money just isn't stretching far enough.

☐   7. I get angry when my spouse makes an error in the checkbook.

☐   8. I get angry when I'm asked to work overtime for the third weekend in a row.

☐   9. I get angry when I agree to go to a friend's house for a cookout when I'd rather play golf.

☐ 10. I get angry when it turns cold and cloudy after two weeks of balmy, beautiful weather.

☐ 11. I get angry when I have to wait over an hour for the doctor although I have an appointment.

☐ 12. I get angry when a long-winded speaker dominates discussion at a school meeting.

☐ 13. I get angry when I step on the scale and notice I've gained thirteen pounds in two months.

☐ 14. I get angry when I'm ticketed for doing 67 in a 65 mile-per-hour zone.

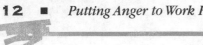

☐ 15. I get angry when the neighbor's cat wakes me at 3:00 a.m. and I can't get back to sleep.

☐ 16. I get angry when I notice all the things that need to be fixed in my house.

☐ 17. I get angry when I spill my soft drink as I try to juggle my three remote control clickers.

☐ 18. I get angry when two co-workers arrive eight minutes late for a meeting.

☐ 19. I get angry when I get voice mail instead of the person I'm trying to reach.

☐ 20. I get angry when I learn what is happening in Washington, D.C.

If you marked "yes" to more than five of these questions, perhaps it's time for you to learn how to put anger to work *for* you instead of allowing it to work *on* you.

HOW DO

You Deal With Your

ANGER?

Many people equate anger with aggression and hostility. But anger is *not* aggression. Anger is an emotion. Aggression is a course of action that a person chooses after experiencing anger.

Somewhere between the stimulus of your anger and your response, there is choice. You can choose to use your anger constructively, or you can choose to abuse it.

Ways to Deal With Anger

There are three main ways people handle anger:

1. Aggression
2. Passive aggression
3. Proactive assertiveness

The United States of Aggression

The reality is that aggression is a common response to anger in America. Crime statistics bear this out. But aggression—whether physical or verbal—rarely benefits the person who carries it out. When you "blow up" at co-workers, friends, or family members, you may get what you want, but you'll damage your relationships in the process.

When you act aggressively towards others, you make yourself at once more isolated and more exposed.

You isolate yourself because others create barriers—they build walls—to counter your aggression. Some people protect themselves with physical distance. Others keep an emotional distance.

At the same time, when you respond aggressively, you expose yourself. Expressing anger aggressively reveals your vulnerable points to others in ways that lead to more hurt rather than more intimacy. In *Atlas Shrugged*, Ayn Rand writes of one of her characters: "He liked to observe emotions; they were like red lanterns strung along the dark unknown of another's personality, marking vulnerable points."

ANGRY "NICE" PEOPLE HAVE MORE "ACCIDENTS"

Don't be fooled by "nice" passive people. Those who try to put a lid on their anger by controlling it or denying it often express their anger in passive-aggressive ways. They believe they are controlling their anger by not yelling or becoming hostile in overt ways. Yet they really do not deny themselves their anger. Not handled directly, anger seeps into your actions below your conscious awareness. When you are angry at your spouse for not coming home on time, you may holler when he or she finally shows up. That is an aggressive response. But a passive-aggressive response might be "accidentally" burning a hole in that person's favorite shirt or blouse with an iron.

People who attempt to bury their anger go about their business unaware that their anger is operating at a subconscious level. They don't see their anger as the real cause of the "accidents," and neither do others.

PROACTIVE ASSERTIVENESS

The third way to handle anger is to be assertive. Being assertive could be called the half-way point between the extremes of aggression and passive-aggression. An assertive person recognizes his or her anger, deals with the emotion privately, and plans appropriate actions to resolve the situation triggering the anger.

You could say that being assertive is being proactive rather than reactive. When you react to events, you allow outside situations to control you. When you are proactive, you take responsibility for yourself.

Try Exercise 3 to gain an understanding of how you typically deal with anger.

Exercise 3:

How Do You Express Anger?

Choose A, B, or C for each of the following questions. Although the situation may not directly apply to you, anticipate what your likely response would be if you were in such a situation.

1. An airline loses your luggage for the second time in a month. You have to purchase new clothing for an important meeting. What do you do?

   A. Yell at the baggage agent

   B. Do nothing and demand extra service from the airline's ticket agents on future flights

   C. Clearly state the compensation you expect for the inconvenience and extra expense

2. Your child gets two Ds on his fourth-quarter report card. What do you do?

   A. Threaten your child with two months of grounding and later regret it

   B. Say nothing to your child but criticize his grooming, T.V. watching, and failure to run out a ground ball in a Little League baseball game

   C. Express your frustration and concern to your child, try to learn what led to the low grades, and determine together whether summer school is needed and how to prevent the same situation in the future

3. Your partner forgets your birthday. What do you do?

   A. Throw your partner's written apology in the trash with a flourish

   B. Show up late for your next date (you forgot, you ran out of gas, you had a last-minute phone call, you had to work late)

   C. Tell your partner how hurt you are and ask whether he or she wants to be reminded before big events

4. You are asked to take a lateral move (which you consider a demotion) and train your replacement, a person fresh out of college, because "you know more about this job than anyone." What do you do?

   A. Tell your boss off

   B. Train your replacement but "forget" to mention several necessary procedures

   C. Ask to meet with your boss and, if necessary, with your boss's supervisor to discuss how you've been treated and what you can do to advance

5. When your landlord fails to fix a leaking toilet, a piece of your furniture is ruined. What do you do?

   A. Storm into his office demanding $500 to replace the damaged article immediately

   B. Leave lights burning or run your air conditioner even colder than normal until you've settled the score (your landlord pays the utilities), pay your rent late, or advise a prospective tenant to find a better place to live

   C. Get three estimates to repair or replace your furniture and write a letter asking for the amount of the lowest estimate

6. Your mother notices you've put on weight since you saw her a year ago, and she mentions it. What do you do?

   A. Tell her later she has more wrinkles around her eyes

   B. Say nothing but eat so little that your mother is hurt

   C. Acknowledge that she is correct and tell her you are happy with your weight

7. The vertical hold on your television goes out just before the start of a program you've been waiting for all week. What do you do?

   A. Hit the set so hard you get a big bruise on your palm

   B. Slam around and "accidentally" interrupt your partner's regular meditation time

   C. Call a friend and ask him or her to tape your favorite show for viewing after you've had your television repaired

8. A mortgage broker assures you he will get you a loan. Based on this and a letter of intent, you make an offer on a house. You lose the house when you are told on closing day that you aren't qualified for the loan because you've been self-employed for only eight months. What do you do?

   A. Leave a series of harsh, nasty messages on the broker's answering machine

   B. Say nothing to the broker but tell many people about the horrible treatment you received, naming the broker and the company

   C. Ask for a meeting with the broker, with the broker's supervisor, and if necessary, with the state real estate regulatory board to voice how you've been treated, what it cost you, and suggestions to prevent the broker from hurting others

HOW TO SCORE:

Give yourself 1 point for every A answer, 3 points for every B answer, and 2 points for every C answer. If you score between 8 and 13 points, you tend to express your anger aggressively. If you score 14 to 18 points, you generally take an assertive approach. If you score 19 to 24 points, you may be using passive-aggressive means of expression.

Explosion, Implosion, or Change?

Do you hold your anger in, turn it loose on others, or find ways to change the situation that made you angry? Your answer may depend in part on whether you tend to be aggressive, passive aggressive, or assertive.

Think of an explosion as what results when dynamite is used to blow up rock. A gas stove that explodes can destroy a house. You also hear the term *explode* used when someone is talking about anger. The words *he's ready to blow up* and *I am boiling mad* acknowledge that anger can destroy. As you know, this is often what happens when you take an aggressive approach.

Implosion is a less familiar term. When a wrecking company wants to blow up a single building in the midst of other buildings, workers set up charges that cause the building to implode, or fall in upon itself. When you repress or deny anger, you damage yourself "inside." This damage is no less destructive than the damage that results from an explosion. The difference: You take the anger out on yourself. Repressed or denied anger often manifests itself as depression, physical illness, or addictive behaviors. The anger is still there—it just masquerades as other things. Recall how passive-aggressive people have more accidents.

The third way to express anger is to make changes. Use the energy of anger to change yourself or your situation so anger is no longer necessary.

If you are angry because your boss expects you to put in overtime with no extra pay, either you can change or you can change your situation. How?

Changing yourself in this scenario involves changing the way you think about the situation. Let's say your salary is $40,000 a year. If you expect to earn that $40,000 by working 40 hours a week, 50 weeks a year, you are receiving $40,000 for 2,000 hours of work. You earn $20 an hour. Change your expectation to 50 hours a week. You now earn $16 an hour instead. Can you live with $16 an hour and less leisure time? If you can, your anger will dissipate—simply because you changed your expectations.

Assume you can't accept $16 an hour and less leisure time. Then use your anger to change the situation. Change your current job situation to one that is in line with your expectations, or change jobs.

But you might say, "I can't change jobs *because* …" or "I've tried to talk to my boss, *but* …" This is where being proactive comes in. Simply identifying the source of your anger doesn't resolve it. Unless you change something, the anger will always be there. In this case, being proactive might involve a long-term solution—for instance, going back to school so you can find a better or different job.

Feeling trapped makes most people feel angry. Being proactive means looking at various options to correct whatever is making you feel trapped.

Nancy, a woman with a mentally retarded adult son, was very depressed. When she stopped to examine her situation, she acknowledged she was angry because she was getting worn out taking him back and forth to the sheltered workshop where he earned a decent wage. She worked nights; he worked days in a different part of town. Besides being angry, she felt guilty about her anger. A counselor convinced her to give herself permission to acknowledge her anger. He encouraged her to see anger as a warning light instead of as something that was wrong with her.

Together they discussed options, including letting the rest of her family know how tired she was and requesting their help. She resolved the situation by paying her 19-year-old daughter to provide transportation (a short-term solution) and by putting her son's name on a waiting list for the bus the workshop provided (a long-term solution). Her acute depression evaporated.

Anger doesn't go away until you change your situation.

Use Exercise 4 to begin taking a proactive approach to a current situation that is feeding your anger.

Exercise 4:
GIVE YOURSELF PERMISSION TO ACKNOWLEDGE YOUR ANGER

1. Describe a situation that makes you angry because you feel helpless and trapped.

   _____

   _____

   _____

   _____

   _____

   _____

2. View the expression of anger as the warning light telling you that you have engine trouble. You wouldn't want to pull the wire or ignore the light, would you? Use the next few lines to express your anger.

   _____

   _____

   _____

   _____

   _____

3. What short-term changes can you make to improve your situation?

   _____

   _____

   _____

   _____

4. What can you do now to prepare a long-term solution?

_____

_____

_____

_____

_____

_____

WHEN
Your Anger Is
CHRONIC

Sometimes even when you make changes in yourself or in your situation, you can't get free of anger. That's because your anger may be more deeply rooted than your present situation.

CAUSES OF CHRONIC ANGER

Some of the causes of chronic anger are:

1. Parental modeling
2. Unresolved events
3. Irrational beliefs

PARENTAL MODELING

It's possible you are angry because that's what you learned to do. Perhaps concrete problem-solving was something you rarely saw your parents model. If this is the case, you need to work harder to learn what is going on before you can put your anger to work. Exercise 5 will help you to identify the way your parents coped with their anger. Do you see the same patterns in the way you handle your anger?

Exercise 5:
WHAT DID YOU SEE?

Complete the chart with "yes" or "no" answers.

1. When your parents got angry, did they most often:

	Dad	Mom
Blow up?	_____	_____
Clam up?	_____	_____
Express anger and work towards a solution to the problem?	_____	_____

2. If your parents were good models, what are some of the ways they taught you to put your anger to work?

_____

_____

_____

_____

_____

_____

_____

_____

_____

_____

_____

_____

UNRESOLVED EVENTS

Sometimes anger stems from unresolved events from the distant or not-so-distant past. In a marriage, for example, many unresolved events can pile up over the years. Left unresolved, they may culminate in a divorce.

Many times the anger we feel from unresolved events manifests itself in other ways. It seems silly to get steaming angry because someone in front of you is driving too slowly. But it happens. If your anger is out of proportion to an event, that's a good indication that "old" anger is operating.

For example, Kim became extremely angry toward her husband, Brent, if he accidentally woke her in the night. She claimed she became angry because she had so much trouble getting back to sleep and was tired the next day. Although superficially her explanation was true, her anger went much deeper. After years of believing that being tired the next day was why she got so angry, she discovered that the rage actually was coming from her childhood. As a child, she had been wakened in the night by her father and brothers, who sexually abused her. She realized she harbored a storehouse of anger she hadn't dealt with. She went into counseling, dealt with her past, and stopped getting angry when her husband woke her.

Another indication you're dealing with old anger is if you aim your anger at the wrong target. For example, someone at work does something that makes you angry, so you come home and kick the dog. As noted earlier, this is the way you may have learned to deal with anger. Your parents or other adults may have modeled it. Or it might be that you weren't allowed to be angry in your family, so you developed a habit of "displacing" your anger.

It takes courage, strength, and commitment to ferret out the unresolved events in your life and deal with them one by one. As long as those events remain unresolved, even if you don't "think" about them, they are an underground stream of anger that never dries up, keeping alive thorny vines that strangle your relationships.

Exercise 6:
IS YOUR CUP OF ANGER FULL?

To get a better idea of the root of your anger, think about your stormiest relationship. Then answer the following questions, keeping that relationship in mind.

1. Describe the most *recent* event you got angry about.

   _____

   _____

   _____

2. Have you resolved it satisfactorily?   ___ Yes   ___ No

3. If your answer to question 2 is "no," what steps can you take to resolve this event?

   _____

   _____

   _____

4. Describe the event that *in the past* has caused you to be most angry at this person.

   _____

   _____

   _____

5. Have you resolved the event satisfactorily?   ___ Yes   ___ No

6. If your answer to question 5 is "no," how can you begin to resolve it?

   _____

   _____

   _____

You may find that resolving the past incident helps you view the most recent event from a different perspective.

IRRATIONAL BELIEFS

Some people have irrational beliefs about themselves or about others that feed their anger. One way you can determine whether some form of these irrational beliefs underlies your anger is to analyze your vocabulary. If you think in "shoulds," "oughts," and "musts," then more than likely you harbor some irrational beliefs that fuel your anger.

Consider whether any of the following irrational beliefs trigger anger in you. Notice that each belief is based on either winning the approval of others, being treated "right," or getting what you want.

1. ***The My Rules or Else Fallacy.*** I judge others by *my rules.* Those who follow them are okay. Those who don't are wrong!

2. ***The Entitlement Fallacy.*** Because I want something very much, I ought to have it—now!

3. ***The Fallacy of Fairness.*** There is an absolute standard of correct and "fair" behavior. People should know it and live up to it.

4. ***The Fallacy of Control.*** I can control the behavior of others—I just need to apply enough pressure!

5. ***The Conditional Acceptance Fallacy.*** If you love me, you'll…, no matter what.

6. ***The Letting It Out Fallacy.*** People who hurt me or don't treat m kindly should be punished.

7. ***The Self-Performance Fallacy.*** People will judge me as a person based on the success of my performance.

In *Anger: How to Live With and Without It*, Dr. Albert Ellis discusses a therapy he developed called Rational-Emotive Therapy (RET). He maintains that understanding and managing anger depends on intervening at the belief stage. A is the activating event, B is your belief system, and C is the emotional consequence. A plus B always equals C. You cannot change A. But you can change B, which will necessarily change C.

Let's look at an example:

    A. My child misbehaves in a restaurant.

    B. My child is misbehaving because I'm a bad parent.

    C. I feel rotten, inadequate, and angry.

You cannot change A.

You can change B to this: It's two hours past my child's normal bedtime. Most children misbehave when they are tired.

How do I feel now? I become more concerned about my child's needs and take steps to get home as soon as possible.

You could not change A, but you did change B, which in turn changed C.

Exercise 7:

ARE IRRATIONAL BELIEFS TRIGGERING YOUR ANGER?

Think about a recent time when you were angry with another person.

1. What did that person do or say?

_____

_____

_____

2. What do you believe that person should have done differently?

_____

_____

_____

3. Which irrational belief were you applying to the situation?

_____

_____

_____

4. How can you change the situation by changing that belief?

_____

_____

_____

5. How do you view this situation differently now that you have completed this exercise?

_____

_____

_____

For some people, poor parental modeling, unresolved events, and irrational beliefs become entwined, making it even more difficult to sort out how much the past is interfering with their present functioning.

DISCHARGING YOUR ANGER

What do you do if you realize you are experiencing chronic anger? How do you discharge it?

There are various methods that can help, depending on your particular situation. Among these are:

- Seeking professional help
- Doing emotional release work
- Feeling your anger
- Shouting
- Finding a physical expression

PROFESSIONAL HELP

If your anger is old, deep, and profound, such as the anger of childhood abuse survivors, consider seeking professional help to discharge it.

The key to discharging old anger is to realize that it's old. You can't go back and change your childhood, so it's not possible to use the anger for change. The second important consideration is to be safe. You don't want to hurt yourself or others. Professional counseling is one way to provide that safe place and to deal with that old anger. Sure, the costs of professional counseling can be high. But what is your anger costing you now? Lost jobs, isolation, loneliness, embarrassment, broken relationships, headaches? What price would you be willing to pay for a new you, free from your all-pervasive, destructive anger?

EMOTIONAL RELEASE WORK

In their book *Facing the Fire*, John Lee and Bill Stott encourage emotional release work. When you do this work, it is important to realize that the father or ex-wife or teacher you are angry at no longer exists. Today that person is a different person; therefore, you must work out your anger with that person in a nondirect manner. In most situations, it's not even necessary to let your "present-day" father, mother, or whomever know that you did emotional release work to resolve events that happened long ago.

Ginny, for example, felt a lot of old anger towards her abusive father. She stuffed a pair of his pants and a shirt with leaves. She took the effigy to a secluded area and kicked it around the field while verbalizing why she was angry with him.

Some people object to a physical release of anger. They claim that it leads to more anger and doesn't relieve anything since the anger just comes back.

FEEL IT

Doing emotional-release work may not completely relieve your anger—at first. But Lee and Stott say that the first step in dealing with anger is to *feel* it. Emotional-release work allows you to do just that. Anger is a very physical emotion. When expressed appropriately, it is harmless. Although old anger may come back again and again, the intervals between when it comes back will lengthen if you allow yourself to express it physically in safe ways. You'll find that you have more and more "free" time—time when you can deal appropriately and assertively with present-day situations. You will not be able to resolve a childhood or a past relationship full of anger in a short time, but you *can* resolve it.

GET PHYSICAL

You can do almost any physical exercise to discharge anger. But you must *consciously* use that activity for the purpose of resolving anger to get the best results. Physical exercise is a good reliever of all kinds of stress, but anger is not just stress. In order to relieve anger with running, for instance, with each step, you must think or verbalize your anger out and away from you. You don't want to rehearse what you are angry about, but you do want to get it out.

SHOUT IT OUT

Sometimes just getting in your car, rolling up the windows, and screaming can expel anger. This is one method you can use to deal with present-day anger arising from a situation that you cannot change.

Some people are afraid of their anger. But no matter how intense your anger is, feeling it and expressing it appropriately will never hurt you or anyone else.

Other safe suggestions for discharging anger are painting, journaling, breaking old dishes, and twisting a towel.

CELEBRATE YOUR VICTORY

After working on old anger, you will get to the point where you are ready to let go of it. At this stage, you might want to celebrate your freedom. You can devise your own way to do that. Write down what you have been angry about. Attach the paper to a helium balloon and release it. Or burn the paper. Or bury it. All of these are symbols of letting go of the anger. Even if the anger returns, a short session of release work and remembering your "letting go" ceremony will restore your emotional equilibrium.

4

HOW TO USE

Anger As a Tool, Not As a

WEAPON

As you've already seen, if you do not deal directly with your anger, it will affect you and your relationships in indirect ways. In this chapter, you'll learn a five-step method for managing your anger and using it as a tool rather than as a weapon.

STEP 1: RECOGNIZE YOUR ANGER

The first step in managing your anger is acknowledging you're angry. Many people don't know they are angry until they blow up. To manage anger better, you must recognize that you are angry sooner.

To some extent, the physical effects of anger are the same as they are for any stress—tight muscles, shallow breathing, increased heart rate. However, certain clues indicate that you are dealing with anger rather than another emotion—clenched fists, pursed lips, and nasal breathing are a few. In fact, the Hebrew word for "anger" is *aph*, which means "nostril."

Instead of openly acknowledging your anger, you may have learned to soften it: "I'm upset," "I'm irritated," or "I'm miffed." Those are low levels of anger, but it's the ideal point to begin exercising control of your anger.

STEP 2: PINPOINT THE SOURCE OF YOUR ANGER

After acknowledging your anger, deliberately open and close your fingers, open your mouth, and breathe deeply. You can do these simple steps no matter who may be around.

Then identify the specific event you are angry about. The more closely you can pinpoint the problem, the more likely you can solve it. (Reread Chapter 1 and review Exercise 1.)

Here are some questions you can ask yourself to identify the source of your anger:

1. What am I really angry about?

2. How is my "self" being threatened or violated?

3. Do I have a valid need that is not being met?

4. Am I frustrated because one of my expectations isn't being met?

5. Do I believe an injustice is occurring?

6. What is the problem, and whose problem is it?

7. Who is blocking my path?

8. Who is not treating me with respect?

STEP 3: POINT OF DECISION

It is at this point that you make a conscious decision to use your anger as a tool rather than as a weapon.

When you use anger as a weapon, you ask yourself questions such as these:

1. Whose fault is this?
2. How can I make another person respect my boundaries?

When you use anger as a tool, you ask these types of questions:

1. What particular boundary has been violated and what do I need to do to reset the boundary?
2. How can I express my anger in a way that will not leave me feeling helpless and powerless?

Notice that when you use anger as a weapon, you focus on the other person. When you use anger as a tool, you focus on yourself. In other words, you "own" your anger and take responsibility for taking care of yourself. You are dealing with anger assertively, proactively. You think, "*I* am angry. What can *I* do about it?" rather than "*You* make me angry. What are *you* going to do about it?"

Why is this distinction so important? Because you can always change yourself and your feelings, but you can rarely change another person. When you focus on yourself, you have power. When you focus on the other person, you are helpless. And remember, feeling helpless only increases anger.

STEP 4: PLAN TO ACT

Aristotle said in the fourth century B.C.: "It is easy to fly into a passion—anybody can do that—but to be angry with the right person to the right extent and at the right time and with the right object and in the right way—that is not easy, and it is not everyone who can do it."

Handling your anger the way Aristotle recommends requires thought and planning, not an off-the-cuff reaction at the moment you become angry. Consider the following example of how one person handled her friend's habitual lateness.

Ginger was angry because her friend was chronically late. Not by a few minutes but by several hours. She owned her anger and analyzed what she was angry about. She concluded that her friend's lifestyle probably wasn't going to change if she confronted her. Instead, Ginger chose to plan activities with her friend that allowed her to use the time she was waiting in a constructive manner. As she loosened her expectations of her friend, she could laugh at her friend's tardiness rather than get angry. She made it a game to see how many tasks she could complete between the time her friend said she would arrive and when she actually showed up.

STEP 5: COUNT THE COST

A wise man once said: No one begins a building or goes to war without finding out how much it is going to cost.

Once you identify a problem and begin looking at solutions, count the cost. What will be the probable outcome if you try different solutions? In *Dance of Anger*, Harriet Learner writes that many times at a subconscious level, women count the cost and then choose not to act assertively, much to the dismay of friends and family.

Likewise, Judith Stone wrote in the July 1993 issue of *Glamour* magazine: "Economic vulnerability and fear of loss make the low-grade pain of chronic anger preferable to emotional clarity, with its potential for upheaval."

Assume you are angry about constant miscommunication at your job. You determine it would be better to have a line of communication clearly set out in writing. You diagram how that communication could be achieved. What if your plan is rejected? What if it threatens someone who retains power by controlling communication within a company? What might be the reaction? Are you prepared for those outcomes?

When you try to identify what you are angry about, one question you must always ask yourself before you act is this: "What might I be risking if I become clearer and more assertive about this boundary?" Perhaps you will be risking a job or a friend. Are you ready to risk that?

If you count the cost and decide it's still worth trying, you need to have some idea of how to proceed. Ideally, your plan will allow you to achieve your objectives with the least amount of risk.

In Exercise 8, put these five steps to work to develop a plan of action for dealing with a current person or situation that makes you angry.

Exercise 8:
WHO AND WHAT ARE YOU ANGRY ABOUT?

1. Does anyone you encounter on a regular basis at work or in your personal life make you angry often? Write that person's name here.

   _____

2. Acknowledge your anger. Open and close your fingers. Open your mouth and breathe deeply. Write about how angry you feel.

   _____

   _____

   _____

3. What are you really angry about?

   _____

   _____

4. How is your "self" being threatened or violated?

   _____

   _____

5. Do you have a valid need that is not being met? ___ Yes ___ No
   Identify the need._____

6. Do you believe an injustice is being done? What is the injustice?

   _____

   _____

7. What is the problem and whose problem is it?

   _____

   _____

8. Have you been inclined to use anger as a weapon or as a tool in dealing with this person?

As a weapon:

a. Have you focused on fixing blame?

_____

b. Have you desired to make the other person do something differently?

_____

As a tool:

a. Have you focused on resetting your boundaries?

_____

b. Have you tried to express your anger in a way that would leave you feeling more powerful and in control?

_____

9. Now formulate a new plan of action using your anger as a tool:

_____

_____

_____

_____

_____

_____

_____

GUIDELINES FOR USING ANGER AS A TOOL

COMMUNICATE, DON'T ESCALATE

If Ginger, in the earlier example, had chosen to confront her tardy friend, then she would have had to ask herself another question: I am angry because she is chronically late, but how can I communicate my position without becoming defensive or attacking her?

DON'T ASSIGN NEGATIVE MOTIVES

Often, your anger escalates because you assign a motive to the other person's action. The problem is, it may or may not be the real motive.

Ginger could have said to herself: "My friend is standing me up because she does not value my friendship." That may be true, and if so, it might be time for Ginger to seek a new friend. However, it's just as possible that Ginger's friend stands her up because she forgets to check her appointment book, or consistently overbooks her schedule, or underestimates how much travel time to allow—or a million other reasons.

USE "I" STATEMENTS

Once you have identified the risks and decide you still want to confront the person, speak in "I" messages.

Not: "I am angry because you are late."

But: "When you are late, I get angry because I'm afraid something dreadful has happened to you."

Or:

"When you are late, I get angry because I feel abandoned. It makes me remember when my mother died when I was 15."

When you communicate only anger, you put distance in your relationships. When you communicate anger and your feelings behind the anger, you bring more intimacy to your relationships.

VARY HOW YOU EXPRESS YOUR FEELINGS

Sometimes, however, you don't want to take the risk of revealing your underlying feelings. It makes you more vulnerable. At work, for example, intimacy is not the goal. Perhaps increased production or the smooth running of the company is the goal. Consider the following example.

Jack was fifteen minutes late for work three days in a row. Brenda, a member of Jack's team, became angry because production was down 10 percent that week. She believed Jack's tardiness was a major factor. She confronted Jack: "When you are late, I get angry because our team performance suffers. I need you to be on time. Is there something we need to do to help you be punctual?"

What Brenda didn't mention to Jack was that her mother was often late and made her feel worthless. But that type of intimacy would have been inappropriate in this work situation, even though a situation from Brenda's past was feeding her anger.

Techniques for coping with angry feelings vary with the setting. Screaming is an appropriate option when you are alone in the car, but not when you are in a sales meeting. In a sales meeting, breathing deeply is more appropriate. You need to have a grab bag of activities you can reach into and use when you feel your anger rising. Breathing deeply, counting to ten, and opening and closing your fingers are just a few. Using these techniques helps you bring the immediate pressure of anger under control and gives you time to make and carry out rational plans.

Exercise 9:
PLAN TO COPE

Complete the chart with ways you can cope with angry feelings both when you are around people and when you are alone.
Be creative!

AT WORK:

In the Presence of Others	*Alone*
1. *Flex fingers*	1. *Write about it*
2. *Press middle finger to thumb*	2. *Tear up paper*
3.	3.
4.	4.
5.	5.

AT HOME:

In the Presence of Others	*Alone*
1. *Curl and uncurl my toes*	1. *Beat the mattress with a plastic bat*
2. *Twist a plastic tie*	2. *Throw a rubber ball against a wall*
3.	3.
4.	4.
5.	5.

REFRAMING

Yet another method for managing your anger is "reframing." When you reframe a picture, you change the frame, the border, or the matting, and it looks as though you have a new picture.

When it is truly impossible or impractical for you to change a situation, you can change the way you perceive the situation; that is, you can change the way you think about it.

The mind is so powerful that it actually defines reality. How you think about a situation is how the situation is for you. Self-esteem guru Jack Canfield has audiences close their eyes and imagine they are standing at the edge of the roof of a tall building. Though reality tells them they are safe in an auditorium, their physiological response matches what they are perceiving. They report dizziness, lack of balance, and fear of falling. Why? Because perception is reality.

For example, your perceptions color the way you respond to your boss. If you think your boss is tyrannical and thoughtless, you will find yourself angry all the time. However, if you think your boss is authoritative and hurried, you will respond to him or her in a more positive manner.

Reframing, then, is simply trying to see the situation from another viewpoint.

Rhonda got angry because her husband put dishes back helter-skelter in her carefully arranged china cupboard. She spoke to him about it, but he continued to put glasses in the wrong place. She didn't want him to stop helping with dishes and household tasks, so she reframed the situation. Every time she saw a glass that was out of place, she thought how great it was to have a husband who helped around the house. She reframed the situation, and her anger went away.

Exercise 10:

REFRAMING

1. You never seem to have enough money, even though you earn $35,000 a year. You are a teacher and believe that your important responsibilities, education, and experience entitle you to better pay. How can you reframe the picture to lessen your anger?

_____

_____

_____

_____

_____

_____

_____

2. Your six-year-old son has a learning disability. You have had a real struggle with school assignments. Other challenges are managing difficult behavior and teaching your child basic living skills other parents take for granted in a six-year-old. You feel angry that you have such burdens to bear. How can you reframe the picture to lessen your anger?

_____

_____

_____

_____

_____

_____

_____

_____

3. Your supervisor insists on sending you to a seminar on managing negativity because she believes you have a negative attitude. You don't want to go, and you resent the fact that you have to. How can you reframe this situation?

_____

_____

_____

_____

_____

_____

_____

_____

_____

4. Now write out one of the situations in your own life that makes you angry? How can you reframe it?

_____

_____

_____

_____

_____

_____

_____

_____

_____

USE ANGER TO PRODUCE CHANGE

So, once you acknowledge your anger and analyze why you are angry, you must deal with the situation as soon as possible. Resolve the situation and be done with it! But this isn't always possible or practical.

Sometimes it's better to handle your anger later, when you can think more clearly or when the timing is more appropriate. If your teenage daughter took your car without your permission and had an accident, you wouldn't rage at her in the hospital emergency room. You'd deal with her misbehavior later.

At other times, you may try every way you know to solve a problem, but without success. You may reframe the situation, but still not achieve relief. In these situations, it's good to use the energy of your anger to propel you toward beneficial changes. Sometimes these changes require time.

Nicole, for example, had not worked outside the home for fifteen years. Her marriage was on the rocks because of her husband's philandering. She chose to put up with his behavior while she went back to school and obtained her doctorate in psychology. When she filed for divorce, she was prepared to support herself.

Or consider Sam. He had tried everything he knew to manage his anger at work. When he did exercises to pinpoint what he was angry about, he discovered that none of the circumstances that were making him angry were in his control. He used the energy of his anger to seek other employment. It took six months, but he was able to find a job in which he was not angry.

Humans detest change. The only one who likes change is a wet baby. Wherever possible, we hold on to old ways, no matter how painful. But when change is needed, anger is truly your best friend. Anger fuels the rockets to overcome your inertia.

As you harness your anger and use its energy, you can do things that you thought were impossible. You can go back to school, change jobs, and even start your own business. Adrenaline allows a mother to lift a car to free her child trapped under a wheel. You, too, can do "impossible" things if you put your anger to work.

EXERCISE 11:
USING ANGER AS A TOOL

Here is an example of a manager who was angry because he was left out of the communication loop. Notice how he handled the situation, and then offer a different solution, one that would have allowed him to use his anger as a tool.

Tim was preparing to give a report at the 4 p.m. board of directors' meeting. The meeting had been changed to 2 p.m., but no one had bothered to tell him. Tim's intercom buzzed at 2:05.

PROBLEM SITUATION

Boss: "Tim, are you coming?"

Tim: "Where?"

Boss: "To the board meeting. We're ready for your report."

Tim: "It was supposed to be at 4 p.m."

Boss: "It was changed. Get down here now!"

Scooping up his notes, Tim scrambled out the door, putting on his coat and adjusting his tie on the run.

Sound familiar? How would you have handled the situation?

_____

_____

_____

_____

_____

_____

_____

_____

SOLUTION

Let's look more closely at Tim's problem.

He has options other than running out the door in a frantic dash to the board meeting.

He can calmly tell his boss, "Give me 15 minutes to print my report and I'll be there."

While the printer runs, he can do deep breathing, crumble up scrap paper, and spike it into the trash can. He can write himself a reminder to find out later where communication broke down. Writing the note frees his mind from worrying about the cause of the problem. He can use all his energy to deliver the best report he can. Then he can deliberately fix his tie, put on his coat, check his appearance in a mirror, and stride to the meeting, visualizing as he walks down the hall how well he will present his report.

Now is not the time to blow up about how stupid, unfair, and inconsiderate it was to change the meeting time without telling him. Nor is it time to find out what, when, and how this happened. These are issues to settle later.

After the meeting, Tim can work toward preventing future problems. He can first go through the diagnostic questions on page 37 to help him focus his anger. Later he will identify where communication broke down and put in place measures to ensure he is notified promptly about changes in meeting times. He might also consider ways he can change his own habits. For example, he can control his schedule so he has important reports ready at least a day before they are due.

DEALING
With the Anger
OF OTHERS

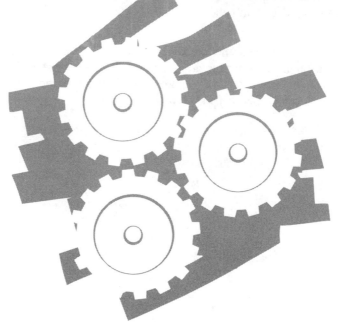

When someone else is angry, it's easy to do one of two things: take flight—run away from the problem—or fight. These are natural reactions. It's easy to respond to someone else's anger with anger. But it's not necessary, and it's usually not productive. If you let the other person's anger become your anger, chances are good that the situation won't be resolved.

A third, and better, option is to de-escalate the anger. When you choose this course of action, you think about the situation and the actions you can take to improve it. This is a response, not simply a reaction. When you simply react, or if you fail to respond altogether, then generally the other person's anger will escalate.

First, look objectively at the situation. Who is angry, and what about? By asking these questions, you can immediately put yourself outside the storm. In essence, you are setting boundaries between you and the angry person.

Next, you need to ground yourself. Imagine you are a tree in a storm. Your roots dig deeply into the soil, and although your branches wave, you are stable.

Just remember, when another person loses his or her cool, it's vital that you don't. Taking a moment to assess the situation before responding to it helps you to maintain your composure. How do you respond to an angry person? The rest of this chapter discusses some effective approaches.

READ BODY LANGUAGE

One of the best ways to tune in to a person's feelings is to observe the angry person's body language. Is the person looking down or away to avoid direct eye contact? Is he crossing his arms or legs to protect himself or to shut you out? Is she tapping her fingers or feet nervously? You might say "You seem uncomfortable with this." Don't comment on specific body movements, just the impression they give you.

Rachel: "Raymond, I can tell you're quite upset about what I just said."

Raymond: "You bet I am. I'm furious."

Speak to the person with a quiet, relaxed, soothing voice. But be careful not to go too far and become "Kindergarten Teacher." If you do, the other person will think you are talking down to him or her.

RESTATE WHAT THE OTHER PERSON SAYS

Show your empathy by restating the angry person's thoughts. As you restate what the person says, be careful not to sound like a mocking parrot.

If you are trying to resolve a conflict between groups of angry people, suggest that the members of each group restate what they think they heard the other group members say they want. Repeat this until all the groups agree that their positions have been stated accurately. When all the parties involved do this, you'll find yourself halfway to solving the conflict. Most important, you will have prevented the group members' anger from becoming your own.

BE CONGRUENT IN YOUR RESPONSE

Studies show that in a face-to-face encounter, 55 percent of what you communicate comes through your body language. Your tone of voice communicates another 38 percent. Only 7 percent comes through the words you speak.

Are you congruent? Do you speak "peace" with your words, but "make war" with your body language and tone of voice? The key is to have peace in your mind, the one spot in the universe you *can* count on. When your mind is at peace, your body language will reflect that.

MATCH SENSORY MODES

Another important technique is to match sensory modes with the angry person. Psychologists, professional mediators, and skilled negotiators do this well.

Basically, we all define and express our perception of the world with sensory words.

I *see* what you mean. (sight)

That *sounds* good to me. (hearing)

Something is not right here, but I can't *put my* finger on it. (touch)

An angry person usually gets locked into one dominant sensory mode. By listening carefully, you can identify that dominant mode. Then match that mode with your speech. You will immediately establish a connection with the person and make that person feel understood.

Practice identifying sensory modes and matching them before you get into an extremely tense situation. You will find lists of sensory words on the next several pages. Become familiar with the words in each category so they'll come to mind quickly the next time you deal with an angry person.

VISUAL

look more closely	3-D
see	vision
show	microscopic
it's a straight shot	perception
see right through	distorted
muddy	blink
flaunt	cover
hidden	find
outside looking in	observation
bright idea	image
spectacle	gaze
pattern	wake up
road sign	reveal
gloomy	blooming
shadow	blind spot
spectacle	window

AUDITORY

on cue	call
turned a deaf ear	pause
same wavelength	discuss
being in tune	tell
sounds good	sigh
pay attention	rhythm
sing out	silence
abuzz	sharply
language	gruff
phrase	term
cry	conversation
hard of hearing	drumbeat
a little flat	words
voice broke	speak
ask	music

Touch (implies "hands-on" or action-oriented mode)

bending over backwards

run with it

rub it in

put my finger on

give it a spin

a pillar

made me dizzy

push

makes

stroke

stable

wear down

drop

supports

crafted

pierce

snub

shape

depth

pull

bend

used

a breeze

spilling out

slump

SMELL

fresh

something fishy here

stuck his/her nose up

clean

breath

fragrance

TASTE

peppered

food for thought

goose is cooked

distaste

steaming

If you cannot identify another's sensory mode preference, rather than mismatch it and escalate the anger, make your response as sensory-neutral as possible.

Not: "I have a clear picture of what you are saying." (sight)

But: "I believe I understand the situation." (sensory-neutral)

USE YOUR BODY

If the angry person is agitated and his or her body movements and gestures reflect this, you can help to produce a calmer atmosphere with your own body movements. Don't match every hand gesture, since that may make the person feel mocked. Move the trunk of your body in a fashion similar to the angry person's and then slow your movements. This will soothe the agitated person. Match your breathing rhythm with the other person's and then slow your rhythm. This will create a calming effect. Remember to be subtle as you match the other person's movements. You don't want to give the impression that you're making fun of the person.

Although all these methods will help you manage the situation by making the person become less volatile, you still must deal with the source of the anger.

ACKNOWLEDGE THE HURT

If the other person has a legitimate beef against you, it is important to acknowledge it and deal appropriately with it.

You might say something like this:

"I can tell you are upset and perhaps hurt over the way I treated you. I am truly sorry."

Don't overapologize, but don't minimize the mistake or suggest that the other person "shouldn't feel that way." "I'd feel the same way if I was in your position" is a lot better than "I know exactly how you feel." Even if you really do, most people believe *their* hurt or anger is unique.

VENTING IS GOOD

In Chapter 3, you were encouraged to feel and express your anger. Make sure you let the other person do that too. It's called venting.

If the other person is very angry and very verbal, you may have to listen for some time as he or she vents before winding down. Anything you feed will grow, including another's anger. If you try to reply before the other person has wound down, you will escalate the situation. Until the other person has wound down, he or she will be unable to hear anything you say, no matter how wise or appropriate. A safe response, if the person gives an opening, is "I can tell you are angry." Don't be dismayed if the person seems to rev up again. It will pass.

Venting can be tough to listen to. But it rarely takes very long. It's usually over in a few minutes. You'll notice that the anger will lessen. Sanity will return.

Most people who've "lost it" in a stormy venting session—venting comes from the Latin word for "wind"—feel other emotions after the storm. Remorse. Regret. Self-reproach ("I shouldn't have done that"). Most will feel sheepish and a little embarrassed.

In other words, the attack is over. In fact, there's been a retreat. The monster who had taken over the other person's mind has disappeared. It's not that the problem prompting the anger has gone. The person has simply let some steam out of the pressure cooker, not turned off the burner. Still, the angry person is now ready to go on to other things. Like solving the problem with your help.

TIME OUT

Sometimes the angry person just needs a cooling-off period. When someone is screaming, hollering, making no sense, or bordering on insubordination, suggest a break.

Go to the restroom. Offer to get the person a soft drink or a cup of coffee. You might need to say: "I want to listen to your concerns. They are important to me. I do need to warn you that the way you are talking right now borders on insubordination. I know you don't want that. Let's pause a few minutes and then get into what's on your mind."

Make sure you let the person know that you aren't trying to put a lid on the issue, that you're just talking about a short break to gather thoughts. If necessary, arrange a specific time to discuss the matter.

SEEK FIRST TO UNDERSTAND

After someone has vented, focus on clarifying the cause of the anger. You might say: "Let me see if I understand." State the situation the way you believe the other person sees it. This encourages him or her to listen to what you are saying. You also give the person the opportunity to comment on your perspective, to make corrections and add input. This in itself often makes the angry person calm down.

Once you've brought the confrontation to the level of conversation, you can ask questions to clarify the situation and enter into the problem-solving stage.

PRETEND IT'S TRUE

Another key to dealing with angry people is to apply Miller's Law. A psychologist, George Miller, said: "In order to understand what another person is saying, you must assume that it is true and try to imagine what it could be true of."

That is, in what situation could the other person's statements be true? When you can answer that, you will know how the other person is understanding the situation.

For example, Jason is listening to his sister, Megan, complain about her new job at the school library. She is upset that reference books are locked up and can be accessed only through the reference librarian.

Megan asserts that as a result, almost no one uses reference books except for special assignments. She maintains that in order to encourage learning, books should be readily accessible, even for browsing.

Jason realizes that what Megan is saying is true about the adult library she had previously worked at. There, the role of the librarian was to be a dispenser of knowledge to responsible adults. At the school library, however, the role is to be an assistant to the youth and the protector of the school's assets. By acknowledging Megan's "truth" and discussing the different roles of librarians, he will be able to communicate more effectively with Megan.

ANTICIPATION AND SCRIPTING

Have you noticed that when you take the time to anticipate what the other person might say in a tense situation and begin with that idea yourself, you may avoid an angry exchange?

Lisa wants to confront Jermaine about the way he addresses her. He calls her "Babe" and "Sugar." Lisa anticipates that when she confronts Jermaine, he might respond, "Get a sense of humor. I wasn't trying to hurt you. I don't mean anything by it."

So Lisa begins her talk with Jermaine with those ideas: "I know you aren't trying to hurt me by calling me 'Babe' and 'Sugar,' and I know you don't mean anything by it, and you probably think I need to laugh about it. But, Jermaine, I feel like you're putting me down when you call me those names. I need you to call me 'Lisa.' Will you do that, please?"

Scripting carries this further. If you've had regular angry encounters with someone, try scripting how these encounters have gone. Now that you've scripted the dialog that usually takes places, read over what you've written. Would you like to change any of your own lines? Make those changes. Rehearse the script by yourself or with someone you trust. When you have your next encounter with the person who makes you angry, try out the new lines. You may find that you begin a newer, better relationship that day.

It really does take two. Change the way you respond and you may find the other person will learn new lines too.

THE POWER OF SILENCE

Silence can be a powerful tool when you are dealing with angry people. Have you noticed that when you say nothing, angry people keep talking? Sometimes, as angry people continue, they may wind down, answer their own objections, and even express regret at having lost their temper.

Don't think you have to respond immediately to everything an angry person says.

DON'T BE A KNOW-IT-ALL

Usually you are not the best person to solve an angry person's complaint. The angry person is. Customer service representatives learn to let a customer vent without interrupting. They show empathy and restate the problem as they have heard it. Then they ask the customer to come up with a solution. "What is a solution you've thought of we both can live with?" Notice the qualifier. You'll be amazed at how reasonable many customers, clients, employees, and family members become when you use this technique. The proposed solution is often one you can indeed live with.

YOUR
Personal Anger
JOURNAL

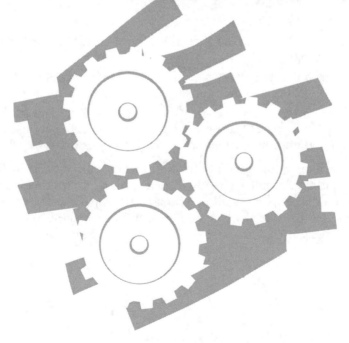

Although anger is a complex emotion, fully understanding its roots, causes, and effects is not necessary for using it effectively.

Remember, anger is your warning light. That is all. The sooner you respond appropriately, the less damaging it is to you and to your relationships.

Start an anger journal using a spiral notebook. Every evening, write about one incident that made you feel angry that day. Be sure to record the details—who, what, when, where, and why.

Then leave your journal for a half hour. When you come back to it, *analyze* the incident.

Ask yourself, in this particular instance, was anger:

- My friend or foe?
- Used or abused?
- Old or new?
- A tool or a weapon?
- Is this a situation I can handle now, or do I need to make long-range plans to deal with it?
- If the incident involved someone else's anger, how well was I able to deal with that person? Did I keep the anger from becoming my own?

Write the answers to these questions in your journal and study them over a period of several weeks. Notice which responses helped you improve a situation, and which ones didn't.

If you'd like, set up a month or so supply of journal pages with your question prompts already in place. Allot two to three pages for each day, enough to allow you adequate space to thoroughly respond to the questions. A sample journal structure is provided on the next few pages.

Remember as you keep your journal that learning to handle anger effectively is not a destination. It's a journey. You'll never arrive at a point in your life where you've found "the way" to handle anger. Every incident of anger is different, involving different circumstances and different people. You'll have to find a new solution to handle each incident. But the skills involved in coping are often the same. Developing them and recording your progress in an anger journal will help you put your anger to work *for* you!

SAMPLE JOURNAL PAGES

A. Description of Incident

_____

_____

_____

_____

_____

_____

_____

_____

_____

_____

_____

_____

_____

B. Analysis

Was anger my friend or foe? Why?

_____

_____

_____

_____

_____

Did I use or abuse anger? Explain.

_____

_____

_____

_____

_____

_____

_____

Was this anger old or new? Explain.

_____

_____

_____

_____

_____

_____

_____

Did I use anger as a tool or a weapon? How?

_____

_____

_____

_____

_____

_____

_____

Is this a situation I can handle now, or do I need to make long-range plans to deal with it?

_____

_____

_____

_____

_____

_____

_____

_____

If the incident involved someone else's anger, how well was I able to deal with that person? Did I keep the anger from becoming my own?

_____

_____

_____

_____

_____

_____

_____

_____

BIBLIOGRAPHY

BOOKS

Bandura, Albert. *Aggression: A Social Learning Analysis.* Englewood Cliffs, NJ: Prentice Hall, 1973.

Canfield, Jack. *How to Build High Self-Esteem.* Chicago: Nightingale Conant, 1982.

Elgin, Suzette Haden. *The Gentle Art of Verbal Self-Defense.* Dorset Press, 1980.

Elgin, Suzette Haden. *Success With the Gentle Art of Self-Defense.* Englewood Cliffs, NJ: Prentice Hall, 1989.

Ellis, Albert. *Anger: How to Live With and Without It.* New York: Carol Publishing Group, 1990.

Friedman, Paul. *How to Deal With Difficult People.* Mission, KS: SkillPath Publications, 1989.

Grandin, Temple, and Margaret M. Scariano. *Emergence, Labeled Autistic.* Novato, CA: Arena Press, 1986.

Lerner, Harriet Goldhur. *Dance of Anger: A Woman's Guide to Changing the Patterns of Intimate Relationships.* New York: Harper & Row, 1985.

Lee, John, and Bill Stott. *Facing the Fire: Experiencing and Expressing Anger Appropriately.* New York: Bantam Books, 1993.

McKay, Matthew, Peter D. Rogers, and Judith McKay. *When Anger Hurts.* Oakland, CA: New Harbinger Publications, 1989.

Poley, Michelle Fairfield. *Mastering the Art of Communication.* Mission, KS: SkillPath Publications, 1994.

Poley, Michelle Fairfield. *A Winning Attitude: How to Develop Your Most Important Asset.* Mission, KS: SkillPath Publications, 1992.

Rubin, Theodore Isaac. *The Angry Book.* New York: Macmillan Publishing, 1969.

Tavris, Carol. *Anger—The Misunderstood Emotion.* New York: Simon and Schuster, 1982.

AUDIOCASSETTES

American Management Association. *How to Handle Anger (Without Losing Your Cool).* Shawnee Mission, KS: Sourcecom, 1987.

Dudley, Denise M. *How to Have Healthy, Happy Relationships.* Mission, KS: SkillPath Publications, 1988.

Sullivan, Nancy J. *Stress Management for Women.* Mission, KS: SkillPath Publications, 1993.

VIDEOCASSETTES

Abiera, Chris. *Assertive Communication Skills for Women.* Mission, KS: SkillPath Publications, 1994.

Arredondo, Lani. *The Essentials of Credibility, Composure and Confidence.* Mission, KS: SkillPath Publications, 1994.

Dahl, Lyn. *Managing Negativity in the Workplace.* Mission, KS: SkillPath Publications, 1994.

Scofield, Carol. *Conflict Management Skills for Women.* Mission, KS: SkillPath Publications, 1994.